Brendan Byrne

Coping with Bullying in Schools

CASSELL

Cassell
Villiers House
41/47 Strand
London WC2N 5JE

387 Park Avenue South
New York
NY 10016-8810

First published 1994
Reprinted 1995

British Library Cataloguing-in-Publication Data
A catalogue record for this book is available from the British Library

ISBN 0-304-33071-X (paperback)

Printed and bound in the Republic of Ireland
by Colour Books Ltd, Dublin

Contents

Author's Note

This book is based on my experience as a school teacher and on a Ph.D. thesis in Education, completed in University College, Dublin, under the supervision of Professor Desmond Swan. I am indebted to him for his guidance and encouragement. Special thanks are due to the principals, teachers, and pupils without whom the study would not have been possible.

Back in the Playground Blues

Dreamed I was in a school playground, I was about four feet high
Yes I dreamed I was back in the playground,
    and standing about four feet high
The playground was three miles long
    and the playground was five miles wide

It was broken black tarmac with a fence all round
Broken black dusty tarmac with a high fence running all round
And it had a special name to it, they called it The Killing Ground.

Got a mother and a father, they're a thousand miles away
The Rulers of the Killing Ground are coming out to play
Everyone thinking: who they going to play with today?

    You get it for being Jewish
    Get it for being black
    Get it for being chicken
    Get it for fighting back
    You get it for being big and fat
    Get it for being small
    O those who get it get it and get it
    For any damn thing at all

Sometimes they take a beetle, tear off its six legs one by one
Beetle on its black back rocking in the lunchtime sun
But a beetle can't beg for mercy, a beetle's not half the fun

Heard a deep voice talking, it had that iceberg sound;
'It prepares them for life' – but I never found
Any place in my life that's worse than The Killing Ground.

Adrian Mitchell (Rosen 1985)

Introduction

In 1984 I had been teaching geography and English for eleven years in a secondary school for boys. In that time I had come across a number of incidents of aggressive behaviour among pupils. In most cases one student was found to be acting aggressively towards another student. Occasionally a group of students were found to be the aggressors. These incidents tended to occur in the corridors, the playground and the area immediately outside the school. Sometimes the exchanges were physical but, more often, they involved name-calling, taunting or teasing.

Serious cases of aggressive behaviour were reported to the principal. Despite this, I sometimes had the feeling that more could be done. There seemed to be no structure in position by means of which the incidence and nature of this aggressive behaviour could be examined and discussed by people in the school who might be in a position to do something about it. If other teachers in the school were encountering such behaviour as often as I was, then it constituted a problem which merited some examination.

In October 1984, I had the opportunity to study for the degree of Master in Education in Trinity College, Dublin. Having decided to specialise in the area of guidance and counselling, I completed a dissertation on the incidence and nature of bullies and victims in a Dublin city post-primary school for boys. There were major limitations to this study in that it examined only part of one single-sex school. The opportunity to look at the phenomenon of bullying behaviour in a range of schools was the impetus to undertake a Ph.D. in Education at University College, Dublin.

Bullying is difficult to detect. It is a secretive form of behaviour about which there is growing awareness. This book is intended as a resource for parents, school principals, and teachers. I hope that it will shed light on practical ways of dealing with this difficult problem.

PART I

The Theoretical Background

Definitions of Bullying Behaviour

Bullying behaviour may be viewed as a form of aggression. Aggression covers a very wide range of activity. Webster's Third New International Dictionary defines aggression as 'an offensive action or procedure: a culpable unprovoked overt hostile attack'. A further definition however is 'healthy self–assertiveness or a drive to accomplishment or to mastery especially of skills'[1]. J. Dollard, L.W. Doob, N.E. Miller, D.H. Mowrer and R.R. Sears defined aggression as 'a sequence of behaviour, the goal response to which is the injury of the person toward whom it is directed'[2]. Konrad Lorenz described aggression as 'the fighting instinct in beast and man which is directed against members of the same species'[3]. Aggression in the context of this book will refer to the negative aspect of the term, i.e. hostility rather than assertiveness.

Delwyn Tattum points out that the term bullying is all-embracing including anti-social acts such as assault, extortion, intimidation and violence. Bullying should be seen on a continuum of severity, but the most important thing is to appreciate in each instance that bullying is a wilful, conscious desire to hurt another person.[4] In a Scandinavian context, Erling Roland says that the following definition of bullying would be generally accepted:

Bullying is long-standing violence, physical or psychological, conducted by an individual or a group, and directed against an individual who is not able to defend himself in the actual situation. The physical bullying could include kicking, pushing, or beating the victim, while the most common means of psychological bullying are teasing and exclusion. [5]

Pete Stephenson and Dave Smith describe bullying as 'a form of social interaction in which a more dominant individual (bully) exhibits aggressive behaviour which is intended to and does, in fact, cause distress to a less dominant individual (the victim). The aggressive behaviour may take the form of a direct physical and/or verbal attack or may be indirect as when the bully hides a possession that belongs to the victim or spreads false information about the victim. More than one bully and more than one victim may participate in the interaction.'[6] This definition focuses on the distress the victim experiences, the abuse of power by the bully, and the intentionality of the act.

David A. Lane includes as bullying behaviour 'any action or implied action, such as threats or violence, intended to cause fear and distress'[7]. Once again the notion of intentionality is central. In a major study in Scandinavia Dan Olweus examined aggression in schools. He defined a bully as 'a boy who fairly often oppresses and harasses somebody else. The target may be boys or girls, the harassment physical or mental.' He has described a victim as 'a boy who for a fairly long time has been and still is exposed to aggression from others; that is boys and possibly girls from his own class or maybe from other classes often pick fights and are rough with him and tease or ridicule him.'[8] It is important to note that Olweus studied only boys, in the belief that bullying behaviour would be confined almost exclusively to boys. His definitions stress the physical and the mental nature of behaviour and the fact that it is going on over a period of time, i.e. the stability aspect. Kaj Bjorkqvist, Kerstin Ekman and Kirsti Lagerspetz see bullying as 'a special case of aggression which is social in its nature' [9].

Sue Askew argues that bullying should be regarded as 'a continuum of behaviour which involves the attempt to gain power and dominance over another'. She says that long term bullying will have painful consequences for the victim but in addition concerns the classroom because a pupil's feeling of safety and for learning is affected by power struggles within the group. Viewing bullying as a continuum of behaviour meant that 'once-off' incidents of verbal and physical assault right up to long term abuse could be included.[10]

In their search for a working definition of bullying behaviour, Tiny Arora and David Thompson suggest that a number of studies of bullying in secondary schools have tended to concentrate on the identification of children perceived as bullies by teachers and their peers rather than looking at specific incidents of violence apart from their identification with identified bullies. They decided to use the children themselves to reach a definition of precisely what constituted bullying. A list of interpersonal incidents was drawn up, friendly and unfriendly, and children were asked to indicate whether they had experienced these incidents once only, twice and more, or not at all during the week immediately before. The following week, the children were asked to examine a list of 'unfriendly' actions and decide if they thought

each constituted bullying with a yes, no, or sometimes indication. Six actions were agreed upon in the following order:
1. Tried to hurt me.
2. Threatened to hurt me.
3. Demanded money from me.
4. Tried to break something that belonged to me.
5. Tried to hit me.
6. Tried to kick me. [11]

L.F. Lowenstein found that teachers tended to confuse bullying with aggression and disruption, putting the behaviours on the same continuum. He asked teachers to observe their pupils and note the following:
1. Physical or verbal attacks on the child or group of children, led by a bully on less adequate or effective children.
2. Causing another child or children physical or psychological distress, as reported by the victim, or observed by a teacher, or reported by a parent of the victim. [12]

This observation was to continue for six months. Lowenstein went on to divide bullying into three types of behaviour: physical, verbal attacks, and more subtle psychological attacks.[13]

A study by Irene Whitney, Dabie Nabuzoka, and Peter Smith refers to the vulnerability of the victim and the fact that they are different because of 'their ethnic origin, class, sexual inclination, or physical or learning difficulties'[14]. A definition of bullying from Japan is very similar to those previously mentioned despite the cultural differences. M. White quotes the National Police Agency as defining Ijime (bullying) as: 'attacks on a particular individual, physical and/or through the force of words, involving threats or pushing, shoving or punching, being shunned by their classmates, psychological pressure continually repeated, resulting in suffering to the victim' [15].

Valerie Besag, points to the following problems: few studies available, the contamination of cross-cultural effects, the differences in terminology and the array of research designs employed. Aware of these constraints she gives the following definition of bullying behaviour; 'the reflected attack, physical, psychological, social or verbal, by those in a position of power, which is formally or situationally defined, on those who are powerless to resist, with the intention of causing distress for their own gain or gratification' [16].

The Incidence of Bullying Behaviour

A major problem in discussing the incidence of bullying is that bullying is not always isolated from other forms of disruptive behaviour. A second problem is that by its very nature, bullying is a secret activity and therefore it may be very difficult to obtain accurate figures on the incidence of the behaviour. Many victims are reluctant to speak up about their situation for fear that it will make it even worse. Pat Foster, Tiny Arora and David Thompson say that the incidence of bullying is generally thought to be under estimated because it is mostly hidden and only infrequently reported to adults.[17]

Most research into bullying behaviour has been undertaken in Scandinavia, pioneered by Olweus and confirmed by Kirsti Lagerspetz and Erling Roland. In Scandinavia a number of national surveys have been carried out. Roland stresses that the findings of different investigations do vary, due to the methods and the definitions used. However, he says that it is widely accepted that at least 5% of the children in primary and secondary schools (ages 7–16) are victims of bullying. It is estimated that about the same number of pupils are involved as bullies. In addition four studies have discovered that about 20% of the victims also act as bullies.[18] This dual category will be discussed in more detail later.

The pioneering work in Britain into bullying behaviour was carried out by L. F. Lowenstein. Lowenstein identified eighty-three children as bullied in fifteen elementary and secondary schools. Lagerspetz *et al.* extrapolated from Lowenstein's material the following figures: at ages 7–11, he found 11% and at the ages 11–16, 2.9%.[19] Michele Elliott, who interviewed 4,000 children about abuse, found that 38% had been bullied by other children badly enough to describe the experience as terrifying.[20] Pete Stephenson and Dave Smith, in a study of primary schools, found major differences in the incidence of bullying between schools but on average, 23% were involved as bullies or victims.[21] In the course of his work on truancy, Ken Reid discovered that approximately 19% of truants had started to miss school because of bullying and continued to miss school for this reason.[22]

In Ireland, very little wide-ranging research has been undertaken into the problem of bullying behaviour in schools. J. Mitchel and Mona O'Moore[23], and myself[24], using similar definitions of bullying to Olweus, found figures of about 5% of pupils involved as bullies and a similar number as victims.

There appear to be definite gender differences in the incidence of bullying behaviour. In Lowenstein's study it was found that there were about twice as many bullies among boys as among girls. Kirsti Lagerspetz *et al.* selected a group of bullies and a group of victims on the basis of peer ratings and found that 13.7% of boys but only 5.4% of girls were involved in mobbing behaviour. Mobbing is where a group of children pick on one or more others. Erling Roland suggests that there are about twice as many victims among boys than among girls, and the figures for bullies are about three times as high as for girls. Because these figures are based on pupils' own answers to questionnaires, Roland feels that they may be misleading. He is of the opinion that girls more than boys may be unwilling to answer truthfully about their involvement in violent interactions. Irene Whitney, Dabie Nabuzoka and Peter Smith discovered in their study that boys tended to be bullied mainly by boys whereas girls were bullied by either boys or girls. Of those who were bullied the majority reported being bullied by either one or several boys. Boys admitted bullying others more than girls did. Boys and girls engage in different forms of bullying. Olweus is of the opinion that boys are more direct, more violent and more destructive in their bullying, using physical aggression or threat. Girls favour the more indirect modes of exclusion and malicious gossip. Thus it may be much easier to identify bullying by boys.

The incidence of bullying tends to decrease with age. Olweus found the incidence of bullying to be twice as high in primary as in secondary schools. There was a general decrease in physical bullying among the older pupils. Roland however says that the percentage of victims decreases with an increase in age, for both sexes. However the number of male bullies remains similar at different age levels while the number of girl bullies declines slightly with increasing age. Pat Foster, Tiny Arora and David Thompson found that about half the bullying incidents involve children of different ages, with the younger one usually the victim.

Two studies have indicated that the incidence of bullying is higher among pupils with emotional behavioural or learning difficulties. J. Mitchel and Mona O'Moore found that

16% of children in primary remedial groups bullied others, compared with 6% in non-remedial groups. In a study of a secondary school, I found 9% in remedial classes compared with 5% in ordinary classes.

Causes of Bullying

Valerie Besag asks if there is a section of our society more prone to using aggression and aggressive means than the culture of our schools accepts as the norm. Several studies have shown parenting practices to be highly influential in controlling or encouraging aggressive behaviour. Besag makes the point that in some of the more impoverished communities, the most vulnerable families are scapegoated and bullied by the more robust. However, she rejects the notion that bullying is a prerogative of the poor and disadvantaged, saying that some of the worst and more distressing and damaging cases in her experience concerned pupils with advantaged, and in some cases, privileged backgrounds. Her conclusion is that bullying is 'not the product of status deprivation or financial disadvantage alone ... such factors are but contributory to the problem of violence in our society'[25].

Family factors seem to be of major significance in the development of the personality of children who are bullies or victims of bullying. J. Mitchel and Mona O'Moore found that 70% of the bullies they studied had problematic family backgrounds, while Pete Stephenson and Dave Smith found that one third of those involved in bullying, both victims and bullies, had difficult family backgrounds. Olweus showed that some children have a more positive attitude to the use of aggression, than the majority of their peers. He went on to isolate the following factors as being significant in bullying behaviour:

1. A negative attitude between parent and child, especially mother and son.
2. Over punitive physical discipline, or inconsistent and lax control.
3. The use of physical aggression which is seen as socially acceptable.
4. The temperament of the child. [26]

Wendy Titman refers to a 'code of silence' among children, which, while it may not be the actual cause of bullying, may lead to a situation where bullying can take place. Many children see it as a matter of honour to be able to keep 'secrets', not be 'tell-tales' or 'tittletattles'. Bullies, victims, and onlookers can all engage in this 'code of silence' with serious consequences. Titman also feels that children who are incapable of dealing with peer group bullying and intimidation will stand little chance of dealing with adults who try to bribe them into keeping a 'little secret'. Here she is referring to the problem of child abuse and the wider implications of the 'code of silence'. [27]

Sue Askew focused on how the school as an institution may unintentionally either reinforce or discourage bullying behaviour. The research was carried out primarily with boys, in single sex boys' schools. The central argument is that the values promoted by an institution will reflect the values of the dominant group in society. It is argued that boys' schools are more explicitly built on 'male' values. She reports that physicality was not only used as a means of intimidation among the boys, but also as a way of making social contact.

Apart from physical aggression, a great deal of verbal abuse was heard. Some men teachers commented on the way in which they thought aggression among the boys reflected the authoritarian structures in the school, and referred to the contradictory situation of a teacher threatening a boy with physical punishment for bullying another boy. Competitiveness appeared to be another major element of the boys' schools. Physical strength and power were also seen as part of stereotypical male attributes, and bullying then is a major way in which boys are able to demonstrate their manliness. The author recommends that the school needs a policy which promotes such values as respect, caring, tolerance, and responsibility for others. This policy needs to involve not only the pupils but also the whole staff.

The phenomenon of bullying behaviour in public schools is considered by Geoffrey Walford. He refers to the system of prefects and fagging which helped to institutionalise bullying in public schools. Flogging was a widely accepted part of schooling, as were initiation rites such as being tossed in a blanket at the ceiling at Eaton, hands being seared with burning wood at Winchester, or being forced to drink a jug of muddy water crammed with salt at Rugby. Two major changes have occurred: the importance of sport has declined and with it the 'roughness and toughness' of the schools. Since the 1960s some of the public schools have become co-educational. Walford suggests that bullying is now a matter of verbal and light physical abuse, rather than heavy physical oppression. However, he says that there is a worryingly high number of pupils who experience bullying. What might be defined as 'teasing' in another school would seem to be often described as bullying here. The reason for this may be that unlike in a day school, there is no escape. In such a closed environment, where a few specific boys become picked out to receive 'mild abuse' it becomes bullying.[28]

Generally, aggression occurs as a reaction to aggression but there is a tendency among the human species to practise aggression where there is no fear of retaliation. A study by D. L. Mosher, R. L. Mortimer, and M. Brebel showed that intense verbal aggression led to more retaliatory verbal aggression than did mild distraction. Weak boys were less aggressive against powerful 'bullies' than against powerful non-aggressive boys, presumably because of differential fear of retaliation.[29]

Brede Foy, writing about classroom aggression, identified four categories of disruptive behaviour:
1. Attention seeking behaviour.
2. Opting-out behaviour.
3. Destructive behaviour.
4. Impulsive behaviour.

Contained in her description of destructive behaviour are references to bullying:
Here we have the student who fights, destroys property, steals, bullies. The aggressor who is the bully feels very powerful and invariably has powerful models from films, comics, etc. These models present bodily strength and the use of expletives as a measure of worth; an oversimplification of the conflict between good and evil, a hero who is all powerful, indestructible; an act of aggression that is slick and dangerous. He tries to impose his norms on students who are weaker, dependent, searching for acceptance.[30]

Tapia showed in a study that there is a relationship between cruelty to animals and bullying.[31] Olweus, in his analysis of bully/victim problems, developed a theory sketch of potentially significant factors. It was designed with special reference to a school class. The first group of factors considered the school setting, i.e. the size and design of the school, the size and composition of the classes, the curricula and the teachers. The results indicated that neither the size of the class nor the number of boys in the class was of importance for the degree of victim/bully problems in the class. In addition, the size of the school, in itself, was not an important factor for the appearance and the degree of bully/victim problems. With regard to group climate, the bully/victim problems were largely bound up with the character of the interpersonal relations among the boys in the class. These interpersonal relations were quite stable over time. The relations to the teachers and to schoolwork seemed to be of minor significance, both for the interpersonal relations and for the appearance and degree of bully/victim problems in a class. Kirsti Lagerspetz *et al.* make the point that it is not known to what extent the amount and form of mobbing is different in schools situated in different surroundings.

Traits of Bullies
and the Victims of Bullying

Valerie Besag proposes several subgroupings from the two categories of victim and bully. Passive victims are children who are ineffectual in the face of attack. These children are described as being fearful, physically weaker than their peers, cautious, withdrawn, and often find it difficult to make friends. A significant number have coordination difficulties. They are often clumsy and awkward. Provocative victims intentionally provoke the antagonism of others. They tease and taunt and yet are quick to complain if others retaliate. In some cases children take on the role of victim to gain acceptance and popularity. They are known as colluding victims. Attention seeking might be the motive for those in the next category – the false victims. These are children who are victims in one situation but bully in another. Children who are bullied at home may often bully at school. As well as the traditional bully group which contains children who are physically stronger, have a positive attitude to aggression and enjoy conflict, Besag refers to a group of 'anxious' bullies. These children appear to have other difficulties, such as problems at home or educational failure. They are less confident and popular than other bullies.

Bullying behaviour is found among children from a very early age. M. Manning and A. M. Sluckin reported the persistence of aggressiveness between three and eight years of age.[32] G.R. Patterson *et al.*, in their study of three and four year-old nursery school children in the U.S.A., observed examples of aggression which involved a victim giving up a toy to an aggressor, running away or crying.[33] John and Elizabeth Newson, in their study of seven year-olds in their home environment, refer to the pleasure which some children derive from bullying, and to the cunning with which they can keep it secret long enough to make a victim's life a misery.[34]

Randall examined the nature, causes and cures of bullying within the infant years. Referring to the fact that bullying is usually defined as having the intention of inflicting injury or distress, it has its onset usually between three and four years of age. At this stage a child can understand the feelings of others. He stressed that there is no typical bully – some are tough, popular and rebellious but others may have learning difficulties or be small and weak and seek to assert themselves by intimidating others. The victims at the nursery and early infant ages tend to be marked out for ill treatment because they look or sound different. Sometimes children who have more toys or better clothes attract jealous bullies. Randall contends that bullying is the forerunner of adult violence and has its roots in unchecked infant aggression.[35]

Pete Stephenson and Dave Smith refer to the Cleveland Project which investigated bullying among schoolchildren over a number of years. Information was collected from teachers of final year primary schoolchildren in twenty-six schools. In terms of physical characteristics the findings were as follows: there were no significant differences between the groups as regards the prevalence of physical defects. Victims were often rated as being 'thin' and as 'appearing different from the rest of the class for example in dress and speech'. Both the victims and the bullies were rated as having poor personal hygiene. The findings indicated that the bullies are the physically strongest of all the groups, that they are active and assertive, and that they are easily provoked and enjoy situations which have an aggressive content. They are not insecure or unpopular. A positive attitude to violence rather than insecurity or unpopularity most likely underlies the situation. The victims were rated as being passive individuals, lacking in self-confidence and being unpopular with other children. They were also rated as being physically weaker than other children. All the children involved in bullying tended to have below average school attainments and concentration. [36]

Kirsti Lagerspetz et al. studied group aggression among 434 12-16 year old children in three schools in Finland. A group of bullies and a group of victims were selected on the basis of peer ratings. The childrens' personality variables were studied with questionnaires. The victims had low self-esteem, were subjectively maladjusted, and experienced their peer relations negatively. The victims were physically weaker than well-adjusted children, and obesity and handicaps were more common among them. The bullies were physically strong, and handicaps were also more frequent among them than well-adjusted children. The bullies held positive attitudes towards aggression, experienced their peer relations negatively, and held negative attitudes towards teachers and peers. They were unpopular among their peers, though not so unpopular as the victims. [37]

Kaj Bjorkvist et al. examined the ego picture, ideal ego picture, and normative ego picture of bullies and their victims in a school situation using semantic (word) differentials. The bullies considered themselves to be dominant, had high ideals concerning dominance and thought this was what the social norms require. They felt themselves to be impulsive and lacking in self control. The victims considered themselves to be depressed, lacking in intelligence and personal attractiveness, and displayed in general feelings of inferiority. These characteristics can be partly a cause and partly an effect of the bullying situation. Girls scored lower in general than boys on socially valued characteristics and higher on socially undesirable ones. [38]

Olweus showed that bullies held positive attitudes towards violence. Their grades in school were average or possibly somewhat below average. They felt unanxious, confident, tough, and on the whole had a positive attitude towards themselves. The bullies were quite popular among their peers, although not as popular as the well-adjusted average boys. The bullies had handicaps more frequently than the well-adjusted. The victims were unpopular among their peers, passive in their social relations, anxious and lacking in assertiveness and self-esteem. The victims in Olweus' study were not deviant in any other respect except that they were physically weaker than the others. [39]

L.F. Lowenstein, having identified eighty-three children as bullies, studied them with observational techniques, interviews and a Personality Inventory. These were compared to non-bullied control children. The data suggested that:

(a) Bullying may be divided into three types of behaviour: physical, verbal attacks, and more subtle psychological attacks.

(b) The most common observable forms of bullying are physical attacks on other children.

(c) There is a greater amount of bullying among boys than among girls.

(d) Girls are more likely than boys to use verbal and psychological types of bullying behaviour.

(e) Bullying children of either sex are more likely to have parents who have: (i) marital problems and conflicts at home (ii) been bullies themselves (iii) a lack of values relating to sensitivity to other people.

(f) Bullies are more likely to be hyperactive and disruptive.

(g) Bullies are more likely to have lower IQs and are likely to be behind in their age in reading – this being a single measure of possibly more universal underachievement.[40]

A later study by Lowenstein indicated that a number of distinct physical characteristics and personality traits appeared to be associated with children who were likely to be bullied. Social skills and the capacity to communicate, being popular and showing interest in others, were features likely to mitigate against being bullied. Children who were physically robust, extroverted, socially sensitive, unselfish, flexible, conforming to group norms, rewarding, unaggressive, non-attention seeking and modest individuals, were less likely to be bullied that those of the opposite trait. [41]

Ken Reid set out to examine the link between bullying and persistent school absenteeism. His conclusion was that bullying is a significant factor in school absenteeism in only a minority of cases. The absentees as victims 'tend to be vulnerable, to have low self concepts, to be defenceless, to exaggerate or to worry about perceived or actual threats, to draw attention to themselves through their behaviour, temperament or personality and, in a clear minority of cases, to invite retribution through their own aggressive stances'. [42]

R.A. Glow and P.H. Glow examined the popularity of bullies versus non-bullies and concluded that bullies on the whole were not popular.[43] While most researchers have not found bullies and victims to be significantly more deviant than their peers, P. Heinemann put forward the 'deviance hypothesis'. It implies that the victim of mobbing is in some respect deviant, or at least perceived as deviant by the attacking mob. Despite conflicting findings with regard to the traits of children involved as bullies and victims, it is possible to isolate certain physical, psychological, personality and behavioural characteristics shared by children in both categories.[44]

The Longitudinal Aspect
of Bullying Behaviour

David Lane contends that acting to stop bullying behaviour can reduce the incidence of later violent criminality because a number of studies show that problems in childhood are reflected in the adult criminal statistics.[45] M.M. Lefkowitz *et al.* found that aggression at age 8 was the best predictor of aggression at age 19, irrespective of IQ, social class or parental models. However, they were not entirely pessimistic about the outlook for bullies. They have been responsible for a major piece of longitudinal research which accepted the premise that aggression is a socially learned phenomenon.[46] The initial goal of the study was to select a representative sample of American children – 7-9 years old – and to investigate the factors that might influence the development of aggression over time. The results of the study yielded a large amount of information about the characteristics of the aggressive child. All the major findings were consistent with the hypothesis that aggression may be learned by a child from his interactions with his environment. The researchers obtained a second set of data when the children reached the 13th grade. Hypotheses developed from the first study were tested by reinterviewing the subjects of the study when they were approximately 19 years of age. The approach isolated certain child-rearing practices and environmental conditions, that appear to be predictors of aggressive behaviour in young adulthood. The findings confirmed that the punishment of the child at home correlated with the aggression of the child at school, i.e. there was 'a consistent manifestation of aggression across time and across situations'. It was also concluded that 'phenotypic behaviour (greater male aggressiveness) is not necessarily immutable. Just as some females can learn to be aggressive, males can learn not to be aggressive.' Thus, seen in light of the social learning theory of aggressive behaviour, propounded by these researchers, the prognosis is that bullying need not be for life. Like most other behaviours it can be unlearned. [47]

D. Lewis cites a long term study undertaken on 800 children in America which revealed that children who bullied in first grade were very likely to grow up into aggressive, antisocial adults. Their marriages were less satisfactory than those of children who were not bullies at that age. They were more likely to use violence against their own children. The had poor personal relationships, with few friends. They stood a greater chance of getting into trouble with the law.[48]

Dave Smith suggests that the peer rejection which victims often experience is a strong predictor of later adult disturbance. He refers to research by Gilmartin which, using retrospective data, found that 80% of 'love-shy' men (who despite being heterosexual found it very difficult to have relationships with the opposite sex) had experienced bullying or harassment at school. [49]

Dan Olweus conducted two longitudinal studies covering a one- and a three-year interval respectively on two samples of boys aged 13 years to examine aggression and peer acceptance in adolescent boys. The results indicated high degrees of stability over time in the dimensions of aggression and peer acceptance.[50]

Valerie Besag feels that bullying is often sustained over a long period of time, being handed on from class to class or even year to year.[51] R.J. Cole found that two thirds of teachers facing the problem of bullying had inherited it from the previous year.[52] D. Riley found that over fifty per cent of bullies had been identified by the feeder schools prior to entering the secondary school.[53] In Scandinavia, Kirsti Lagerspetz *et al.* reported a ninety three per cent stability of incidence over one year. [54]

1   Webster's Dictionary (1966), New York: Harbor House

2   Dollard, J., Doob, L.W., Miller, N.E.; Mowrer, D.H. and Sears, R.R. (1939) *Frustration and Aggression*, New Haven: Yale University Press.

3   Lorenz, K. (1966) *On Aggression*, New York: Harcourt, Brace and World, p IX

4   Tattum, D. (1989) 'Violence and Aggression in Schools', in D. Tattum and D. Lane (Eds.), *Bullying in Schools*, Stoke-on-Trent: Trentham Books, pp 7-19

5   Roland, E. (1989) 'Bullying: The Scandinavian research Tradition', in D. Tattum and D. Lane (Eds.), *Bullying in Schools*, Stoke-on-Trent: Trentham Books, pp 21–32

6   Stephenson, P. and Smith, D. (1988) 'Bullying in the junior school', in D. Tattum and D. Lane (Eds.), *Bullying in Schools*, Stoke-on-Trent: Trentham Books, pp 45–57

7   Lane, D.A. (1989) 'Violent Histories: Bullying and Criminality', in D. Tattum and D. Lane (Eds.), *Bullying in Schools*, Stoke-on-Trent: Trentham Books, p 96

8   Olweus, D. (1978) *Aggression in the Schools: Bullies and Whipping Boys*, Washington D.C.: Hemisphere

9   Bjorkqvist, K., Ekwan, K., Lagerspetz, K. (1982) 'Bullies and victims: their ego picture, ideal ego picture, an normative ego picture', *Scandinavian Journal of Psychology*, 23, pp 307–313

10 Askew, S. (1989) 'Aggressive behaviour in boys:to what extent is it institutionalised?', in D.Tattum and D.Lane, *Bullying in Schools*, Stoke-on-Trent: Trentham Books, pp 59–70

11 Arora, C.M.J. and Thompson, D.A. (1987) 'Defining bullying for a secondary school', *Education and Child Psychology*, 4(3)4, pp 110-120

12 Lowenstein, L.F. (1978a) 'Who is the bully?' *Bulletin of the British Psychological Society*, 31, pp 147–149

13 Lowenstein, L.F. (1978b) 'The bullied and the non-bullied child', *Bulletin of the British Psychological Society*, 31, pp 316-318

14 Whitney, I., Nabuzoka, D. and Smith, P.K. (1992) 'Bullying in Schools: Mainstream and special needs', *Support for Learning*, vol 7, No 1, pp 3–7

15 White, M. (1987) *The Japanese Educational Challenge*, London: Free-Press/MacMillan

16 Besag, V.E. (1989) *Bullies and Victims in Schools*, Milton Keynes: Open University Press, p 4

17 Foster, P., Arora, T., and Thompson, D. (1990) 'A whole-school Approach to Bullying', *Pastoral Care*, September, pp 13–17

18 Roland, E. (1989) 'Bullying: The Scandinavian Research Tradition', in D. Tattum and D. Lane (Eds.), *Bullying in Schools*, Stoke-on-Trent: Trentham Books, p 22

19 Lagerspetz, K.M.; Bjorkquist, K.; Berts, M.; and King, E. (1980) 'Group aggression among school children in three schools', *Scandinavian Journal of Psychology*, 8, pp 45–52

20 Elliott, M. (1986) *Kidscape Project*, The Kidscape Primary Kit, Kidscape, 82, Brock Street, London W1Y 1YP

21 Stephenson, P. and Smith, D. (1988) p 47

22 Reid, K. (1984) 'Disruptive behaviour and persistent school absenteeism', in N. Frude and H. Gault (Eds.), *Disruptive Behaviour in Schools*, Chichester: John Wiley, pp 77–98

23 Mitchel, J. and O'Moore, M. (1988) in *Report of the European Teachers' Seminar on Bullying in Schools*, Strasbourg: Council for Cultural Cooperation

24 Byrne, B. (1987) A study of the nature and incidence of bullies and whipping boys (victims) in a Dublin City post primary school for boys. Unpublished M.ED. thesis, Trinity College, Dublin

25 Besag, V. p 38

26 Olweus, D. (1980) 'Familial and temperamental determinants of aggressive behaviour in adolescent boys: A causal analysis', *Developmental Psychology*, 16, pp 644–660

27 Titman, W. (1989) 'Adult Responses to Children's Fears: Including Resource materials', in D. Tattum and D. Lane (Eds.), *Bullying in Schools*, Stoke-on-Trent: Trentham Books, pp 105-116

28 Walford, G. (1988) 'Bullying in Public Schools: Myth and Reality', in D. Tattum and D. Lane (Eds.) *Bullying in Schools*, Stoke-on-Trent: Trentham Books, pp 81–88

29 Mosher, D.L.; Mortimer, R.L.; and Brebel, M. (1968) 'Verbal Aggressive Behaviour in Delinquent Boys', *Journal of Abnormal Psychology*, 73, pp 454–460

30 Foy, B. (1977) 'Classroom Aggression', *International Review of Education*, UNESCO, 23, pp 97–118

31 Tapia, F. (1971) 'Children who are cruel to animals', *Child Psychiatry and Human Development*, 2, pp 70–77

32 Manning, M. and Sluckin, A.M. (1984) 'The function of aggression in the pre-school and primary years', in N. Frude and H. Gault (Eds), *Disruptive Behaviour in Schools*, Chichester: John Wiley, pp 43–56

33 Patterson, G.R., Littman, R.A., and Bricker, W. (1987) 'Assertive

Behaviour in Children: A step toward a theory of aggression', *Monographs of the Society for Research in Child Development*, 32, No. 5, pp 161–166

34   Newson, J. and Newson, E. (1976) 'Day to day aggression between parent and child', in N. Tutt (Ed.), *Violence*, London: HMSO

35   Randall, P. (1991) 'Bullies and their Victims', *Child Education*, March, pp 50-51

36   Stephenson, P. and Smith, D. (1989) pp 50-51

37   Lagerspetz *et al.* (1982)

38   Bjorkvist, K *et al.* (1982)

39   Olweus, D. pp 109-117

40   Lowenstein, L.F. (1978a) p 149

41   Lowenstein, L.F. (1978b) p 318

42   Keid, K. (1989) p 93

43   Glow, R.A. and Glow, P.H. (1980) 'Peer and self-rating: Children's perception of behaviour relevant to hyperkinetic impulse disorder', *Journal of Abnormal Child Psychology*, 8, pp 471–490

44   Heinemann, P. (1972) *Mobbning. Gruppvåld bland barn och vuxna*, Stockholm: Natur och Kultur

45   Lane, D. (1989) p 95

46   Lefkowitz, M.M.; Eron, L.D.; Walder, L.O.: and Huesmann, R. (1977) *Growing Up to be Violent*, New York: Pergamon Press

47   Eron, L.D., Walder, L.O., and Lefkowitz, M.M. (1971) *Learning of Aggression in Children*, Boston: Little Brown

48   Lewis, D. (1988) *Helping your Anxious Child*, London: Methuen

49   Smith, P.K. (1991) 'The Silent Nightmare: Bullying and Victimisation in school peer groups', *Bulletin of the British Psychological Society*, 4, pp 243–248

50   Olweus, D. (1979) 'Stability of aggressive reaction patterns in males: A review', *Psychological Bulletin*, 86 (4), pp 852–875

51   Besag, V. (1989) p 13

52   Cole, R.J. (1977) The Bullied Child in School. Unpublished M. Sc. dissertation, University of Sheffield

53   Riley, D. (1988) Bullying: A Study of Victims and Victimisers within one inner city secondary school. In-service B. Ed. inquiry report, Crewe and Alsager College of Higher Education

54   Lagerspetz, K. *et al.* (1982)

Sticks and stones may break my bones,
but words can also hurt me.
Sticks and stones break only skin,
while words are ghosts that haunt me.

Slant and curved the word-swords fall
to pierce and stick inside me,
Bats and bricks may ache through bones,
but words can mortify me.

Pain from words has left its scar
on mind and heart that's tender.
Cuts and bruises now have healed;
it's words that I remember.

PART II

Bullies and Victims in Schools:
Author's Findings

Bullies and Victims in Schools

Bullying refers to an on-going systematic pattern of behaviour. It lasts for weeks, months and even years. Therefore it does not include isolated incidents. Bullying may be physical or mental or a combination of both. All bullying has a psychological effect. Both boys and girls can be involved in bullying behaviour, though usually in different ways. A person may be a victim of bullying by one other person or by a group. Whether a person is a bully or a victim is the result of the complicated interaction of a number of factors.

Family Background Features

There is a trend which suggests that first children are more likely to be victims at school than later children in a family. This raises questions about whether child-rearing practices are very different for first children. In some cases, first children may be over-protected. Inexperienced and conscientious parents may be more reluctant to allow them to be independent when compared with later children. This may increase the likelihood that first children will be less integrated into the class group.

An examination of social background also highlights some interesting differences. Victims tend to have parents who are friendlier. The victims tend to come from roughly the same social background as the norms for the school. This is not generally true of the bullies. Neither bullies nor victims tend to come from homes where there is a balanced attitude to child-rearing. Often victims are over-protected, while bullies frequently have aggressive, dominant parents.

Gender differences

Boys are more likely to be involved in bullying behaviour than girls. Physical bullying and extortion are more common among boys than girls. A common form of bullying among girls is exclusion. This practice can last for weeks or months and is usually orchestrated by one or two ringleaders with the general class group joining in behind them. In co-educational schools, boys tend to be bullied by boys. Girls tend to be bullied by either boys or girls or both.

Physical Characteristics

Physical characteristics have been considered to be of great importance in determining whether or not a person might be a bully or a victim. It is probably true to say that some male bullies, especially in primary schools, are physically bigger and stronger than the average. This would be less often the case in secondary schools or in relation to girls. It seems to me that many bullies, while not actually physically bigger and stronger, have the ability to project themselves as big people. They do this by means of very aggressive body language. The voice can also be used in this way and what is referred to by students as the 'look'. Very often the victim is harassed by means of intimidation rather than the use of actual physical force.

The stereotype view of the victim is that they often have a physical peculiarity, e.g. very small or weak, fat or thin, wear glasses, stutter or stammer. However, I prefer to see these physical characteristics as triggers but not necessarily important on their own. Not all people who wear glasses or who are fat or very small will be victimised at school. However, if a person has one of the physical characteristics previously mentioned and a particular type of personality and certain family background features it is likely that they may be bullied. We are moving toward the idea of a package and a distinctive physical characteristic may be seen as the trigger in this context.

Psychological Traits and Personality Characteristics
It is to be expected that victims will have lower self esteem than bullies and average children. This is in fact the case and is the result of persistent harassment either physical or mental. However, it is also the case that bullies have lower self esteem than average children. Any attempt to help the bully should seek to find the cause of this low self esteem.

The manner in which a person relates to others may be seen as a key factor in bully/victim problems. Compared to victims, bullies are more extroverted, outgoing and capable of rapport with others. Victims are more obedient, mild, easily led, accommodating and submissive than the bullies. The bullies are more assertive, competitive, aggressive, stubborn and dominant. The victims are more sober, taciturn and serious while bullies tend to be enthusiastic, heedless and 'happy-go-lucky'. Victims are shy, timid and threat-sensitive while the bullies are adventurous 'thick-skinned' and socially bold. Bullies tend to be sociably group-dependent. They are 'joiners' and followers of the group. This ties in with the notion of the 'gang' which is common in many schools. Victims or the other hand tend to be isolated. Many victims give the impression of being independent and unfriendly. This is often the result of being shy and anxious and having poorly developed social skills. However, it is interpreted by the group as rejection. Con-sequently, the victim has no support group if problems do arise. Even students not directly involved in bullying are unlikely to stand up for a person who is perceived as being unfriendly. Some of those who do take part in the bullying, even in a minor way, are happy that someone else is the focus of attention. This raises the question of whether or not the bully is really popular. In primary schools, bullies, especially boys, enjoy a status due to their ability to control the group. However, in secondary schools bullies tend not to be popular. Bullies by this stage often confuse leadership with dominance.

A much less common type of victim is the so called 'provocative victim'. These children seem to bring trouble on themselves by being excessively attention seeking. They may have a habit which is particularly off-putting, e.g. eating habits. The end result is negative attention from one or more in the class group. The provocative victim, because of the nature of his/her behaviour is usually picked on by a number of people, sometimes even the whole class. Once again this is known as 'mobbing'. Sometimes children whose behaviour would not be considered provocative are the victims of 'mobbing'. However, in such cases, the behaviour is usually instigated by a single bully.

In some classes a child may be victimised because they are academically successful. The prevailing atmosphere in some class groups may dictate that this is unacceptable. Children like this are called 'swots'. The dilemma they face is one of lowering their own standards in order to conform and so achieve a level of acceptance within the class group, or continue to achieve and so be the focus of negative attention. This form of victimisation is more likely to occur in mixed-ability classes rather than in rigidly streamed classes.

There are some students who display the characteristics of both bullies and victims. This suggests that they take on the role of either bully or victim depending on the circumstances. For example, a student may be a victim in his/her own class and be powerless to do anything about it. They may displace the frustration they feel in this situation by bullying somebody else, perhaps younger or smaller than themselves.

Name-calling can be one of the most upsetting forms of bullying. The constant repetition of an insulting or hurtful name can have a severe effect on self esteem. Most people will be called names without ill effect. However, when an individual with a high level of sensitivity and a vulnerable personality is subjected to this over a long period of time the effect can be devastating.

'Slagging' is a term often used by students. Usually it implies good fun. However, in some instances it refers to hurtful remarks about physical appearance or about family members, often with a sexual innuendo. The vast majority of students interviewed considered persistent slagging to be a form of bullying.

In primary school, the playground is often the scene of bullying behaviour. Many children who are being bullied will make excuses to stay in classrooms at break-times, but will still have to face the playground from time to time. Common also in the playground is a form of behaviour known as 'mobbing'. Often children from a higher class will seek out younger children than themselves. Boys are often involved in a physical way while girls tend to engage in name-calling, teasing and taunting. In secondary schools, particularly at the beginning of the school year, older students often pick on the new first years. Many see this as a kind of 'initiation rite' but it is really a form of bullying. In boys' schools it is usually physical in nature – jostling and pushing in corridors, locking in toilets, etc.. A similar phenomenon on a more on-going basis is inter-class conflict, again based on differences in ages and physical prowess, e.g. fifth years picking on third years.

Sometimes, the bullying in school may be part of a continuous pattern of behaviour, where the victim is bullied outside the school as well. 'Outside' would refer to the area in the immediate vicinity of the school or the local neighbourhood shops. This continuous bullying of a victim will be most common where the school draws the majority of students from a local area. In this situation the journey to and from school can become a most frightening and intimidating experience for a victim.

It is possible that the coincidental mixture of individuals in a class can be a major factor in the appearance of bullying behaviour. If there is a potential bully in a class it is probable that he/she will seek out a victim in the group. If no suitable person is present in the class, the bully will look elsewhere for a victim. However, if there is a potential victim present and the bullying persists, it suggests that this individual has a combination of physical, personality, psychological, and behavioural characteristics which makes him/her a victim. The manner in which they have been reared, and the school atmosphere, may also be contributory factors.

PART III

Teacher and Pupil Perception of Bullying Behaviour

This section concentrates on the responses of principals and teachers to questionnaires concerning the problem of bullying behaviour in schools. The part which deals with student perception is the result of a structured interview with bullies, victims and students who were neither bullies nor victims.

Principals

Perception of Bullies

The principals' descriptions indicate that there is no typical bully. However, it is possible to group together certain characteristics. The home background is frequently referred to as a major factor. There are references to 'disturbed backgrounds', and 'violent backgrounds'. One principal refers to many bullies also being victims, 'who are threatened and who know no other means of defence.' Some bullies may be attention seekers. Others may be strong, assertive and 'preoccupied with their own needs'. Many are 'unaware of the hurt they cause'. Some points referred specifically to school. One principal said that many bullies 'may have disciplinary problems in school'. Another that bullies 'were often frustrated with school'. There was a reference to 'little motivation'. Similar to this was a point about 'lack of interests'. Overall, there is an impression that principals do not blame bullies out of hand for their behaviour and that they are well aware of causative factors outside the control of the child.

Perception of Victims

The descriptions suggest that there is a 'willing' and an 'unwilling' victim. The first type invites attention, even if it is negative. More common is the victim described as 'quiet', 'meek', 'withdrawn', 'introverted', the 'easy target'. Some victims tend to be 'sensitive' or 'spiritual'. Common characteristics are low self esteem and a lack of self-confidence and social skills. Once again, the influence of home background is seen as very significant. Many victims are considered to be 'over-protected'. Others are dominated at home and are well used to 'adult bullying' and are often timid as a result. The word 'powerless' was used a number of times.

Further comments of School Principals
This section of the questionnaire produced a number of interesting insights. One principal referred to a lack of understanding by fellow students as to why the victim does not stand up for himself/herself. Related to this is the opinion of another principal that all children need to be actively involved in stopping bullying. In a school where the principal has encountered few instances of bullying, the following reason is suggested: 'The children come from various locations – only one third are living locally, and therefore do not meet outside of school hours – nor can the parents take part in the peer battles.' Finally, another principal describes how for the past three years he has had an anti-bullying campaign in the school. He says that physical bullying is practically eliminated, but there has been less success with the elimination of psychological bullying. He says, 'psychological bullying is difficult to discern and often difficult to prove.' Perhaps this is the essence of the problem.

Teachers

Teacher Training

Very few teachers feel that their teacher training adequately prepared them to deal with the problems of bullying behaviour. The teachers have very definite suggestions about how the situation might be remedied both in the course of teacher training and for practising teachers. The emphasis in both situations should be on practical ways to deal with the problem. A number of teachers suggested including a section on bullying in schools as part of the psychology course at training college or university. There were a number of references to the use of role play in this course. For example, it was suggested that the situation of interviewing the bully and the victim could be examined using this technique.

It is a common fear among teachers that intervention by them into a bullying situation may aggravate it. To give them the confidence to intervene in a useful way they point to the need for practical guidelines to help identify children who are either bullies or victims. One teacher stated 'We have nothing to go on at the moment.' Many teachers referred to the need for inservice days to give information on the topic. There was a further suggestion that maybe the Department of Education would devise a general policy on discipline with specific regard to bullying.

Perception of Bullies

There is a definite consistency between the opinions of primary and secondary teachers. Many of the ideas of the principals are echoed. Many bullies have a well developed facility for spotting weakness in their victims. Aggression is a frequent weapon and physical superiority is common. One teacher talks about the 'forceful presence' of some bullies. The following words were used to describe the personalities of the bullies: 'thoughtless', 'loud', 'socially ill at ease', 'insistent on their own way', 'attention seeking'. Lack of confidence was cited as a common characteristic and linked to this was low self esteem. Very often the bully was seen as compensating through his/her behaviour for some weakness in himself/herself. By and large bullies are not popular. One teacher also suggested that their popularity dwindles as they progress through the school. Bullies tend not to have real friends but rather 'hangers-on'. For a lot of bullies the group or gang is all important; 'they are dedicated to the "pack", predatory when safe with the group, but terrified when confronted strongly by a teacher'. Once again there were references to no real outlets or pastimes. The influence of the home background was mentioned repeatedly. One such comment described the bully 'sometimes reacting to being a victim himself in the home or neighbourhood situation.' Aggression in the home often leads to aggression in school.

Perception of Victims

Victims tend to be different in some way from the norm. This difference could be in physical appearance, personality trait or social background. Physical characteristics such as small size or obesity can act as triggers for victimisation. Defects such as imperfect sight (glasses) stammering or stuttering can have a similar effect. Sometimes coming from a single parent family can be a problem in this context. In terms of personality victims tend to by shy, sensitive and fearful. They have difficulties socialising and are described as 'loners', 'isolated', 'outcast'. They tend to be unpopular and in primary school have great difficulty in making and keeping friends. Sometimes they try too hard to become part of a group and rejection leads to even further isolation. When subjected to either verbal or physical abuse most victims behave in a non-retaliatory way. They are afraid to complain and are terrified of being seen as a 'rat'. Academic ability can be an important factor in determining if one will be a victim. At one end of the scale poor academic ability can be a cause while at the other being exceptionally good academically can cast a student in the role of 'swot'. This will apply particularly where the norms of the class determine that it is unacceptable to succeed academically. Some teachers are of the opinion that parents can cause their child to be victimised by over-protecting them, so preventing them developing a sense of independence. Finally, teachers felt that only a small number of victims were attention seekers who brought their problems on themselves.

Bullying in Class

Sometimes, but not often, a pupil will tell a teacher if he/she or someone else is being bullied. The major deterrent here is the fear of being called a 'rat'. There are other less obvious indicators that it is going on. A usually quiet child may become even more withdrawn. Some children, normally restrained, may become aggressive as a result of frustration in failing to cope with victimisation. There may be deterioration in school performance or level of concentration in class. At break time a victim will hang back, reluctant to go to the yard. A child who has been well all day may develop an illness just prior to the break. A child may look distressed and upset after the break.

A victim may be excluded in a number of ways. People may be reluctant to sit beside them. In pair work nobody wants to work with them. At P.E. they are usually the last to be picked for a team by their peers. The group dynamics in the classroom may be a tell-tale sign. The victim is often reluctant to answer questions. When they do there are sneers, sniggers, and knowing glances between members of the class, 'glances of complicity passing between "messers", "assistant bullies" deferring to the "head bully".' Victims are also very reluctant to receive praise from teachers. They may change their seat frequently in an attempt to escape the attentions of the bully/bullies.

The personal property of victims may go missing for periods of time or be damaged on a regular basis. Bags, books, pens, clothes, sports 'gear' are all subject to this. Finally victims may be absent from school without convincing explanation.

When it came to taking steps to deal with bullying going on in their class two different approaches were suggested. Most teachers thought it better to approach the bully and the victim separately and attempt to get both sides of the story. A smaller but significant number of teachers preferred to discuss the matter with the entire class group first, in an attempt to draw attention to the wrong-doing of the bully and so engender support for the victim. It was widely held that in serious cases, both the principal and the parents of the bully and victim should be consulted.

Further comments of the respondent teachers

In this section a number of teachers referred to the fact that bullying goes on unknown to the teacher. It only comes to the teacher's attention when there is a serious incident. Related to this is the point that a lot of bullying goes on outside the school – on the way to and from school, at the neighbourhood shops.

Pupil Interviews

The intention in these interviews was to obtain information on the issue of bullying in schools. The early questions were designed to help the student relax. The bulk of the interview concentrated on pupil attitudes to fighting, their perception of people who are bullies and victims and bullying behaviour. Bullying behaviour referred to saying what it is, where it happens in schools and whether or not anything can be done about it. The children who emerged as bullies and victims in the sample schools were interviewed. In each school students who made up a control group were interviewed. These were students who were neither bullies nor victims. This helped to deflect attention from the bullies and the victims and also gave useful information from the point of view of children not directly involved.

Attitude to Fighting
A number of the bullies referred to the notion of 'mess fights'. They felt that there was no harm in these and that they were 'good fun'. Many were described as being of an impromptu nature occurring between classes, in the corridors or in quiet parts of the yard. Usually these fights involve a number of people but often it is the same people who tend to be on the 'wrong end' of things. It will be seen later that many of the control students believed that bullies

are not always deliberate in their intention to cause hurt. Perhaps a 'mess' fight which is fun to the bully is extremely painful to a victim.

Bullies expressed the view generally that if the situation warranted, they were quite prepared to take physical action. It is of interest that most control students concurred with this view. Victims on the other hand shy away from physical conflict, using words such as 'horrible', 'awful' to describe it. Some of them referred to the fear they had of hurting others should they lose control of their temper. They were afraid that teachers or the principal might see them as the aggressor.

Perception of Victims
In the interview the pupils were asked how they would describe people 'who get picked on'. This was considered broad enough to allow respondents to refer to any of the various characteristics which might apply. The word victim was deliberately avoided in case children who had been victimised would feel uncomfortable. In spite of the fact that the students interviewed ranged in age from eleven to sixteen and were drawn from primary and secondary schools, they referred repeatedly to the same characteristics.

Physically, people who are picked on were frequently described as 'weak' or 'seeming weak to others'. They are often different in physical appearance from the average person, e.g. small, fat. Sometimes a physical deformity or a problem with speech (stutter, stammer) or poor eyesight can be a characteristic. There was a general belief that they are unable and/or unwilling to fight back when attacked physically. Their attitude to aggression is very negative. They do not like fighting or possess fighting skills. The word 'softies' was often used to describe them especially in primary schools. A sizable number of students referred to the fact that people who are picked on tend not to be good at sports and seldom join in games.

In terms of personality people who are picked on are often shy. The most commonly used words to describe them were 'quiet' and 'different'. They are quiet in the sense that they do not react or respond to slagging. They do not complain. They mind their own business. They are 'easy prey'. They like being on their own and are not 'one of the crowd'. Their personality tends to make them seem aloof, independent and largely indifferent to others. Sometimes they give the impression of rejecting the rest of the class and are often unpopular as a result. Socially they tend to be isolated with few friends. Poorly developed social skills allow for little change. When they are picked on there is little support for them within the class group. Occasionally, a person may be picked on if they try too hard to become part of a group within a class. Sometimes they may go so far as to deliberately misbehave in class in an attempt to get 'in' with the group.

Academically, the people picked on seem to be at two extremes. First, there are those who are singled out because they are 'slow' or 'weak' academically. However, a much larger group are those who are known as 'swots' or 'brainboxes'. Related to this is the notion of never being in trouble or being too close to the teacher(s). A number of students referred to the fact that teachers may cause problems by singling out the same person to do jobs (in primary schools) or by praising a very good student too frequently.

Lack of personal hygiene can be a trigger to being picked on in some instances. A further less common occurrence is where there are groups from very different socio-economic backgrounds in the same school. Sometimes a pupil who is perceived as being very poor may be picked on by members of the 'privileged' group. They may stand out because of the poor quality of their clothes or their accent. This type of victimisation can also work the other way around. It is determined by the numbers of each socio-economic background in the class. Where there is a definite imbalance problems are more likely to occur. Sometimes it operates on a group rather than an individual basis. A very small number of students referred to the situation where a person of a different colour or culture might be singled out. It is probable that in multi-racial societies the occurrence is higher.

Perception of Bullies
Having asked about the people who are picked on the next question referred to the fact that there are also people we would call 'bullies' and asked what they are like and why they behave as they do.

There were surprisingly few references to the actual physique of bullies. Some students did say that the bullies are bigger but more often 'bigger' was used to describe how the bullies projected themselves. Expressions such as 'full of themselves', 'swell-heads', 'the men of the class', 'love themselves', 'acting big' refer to this notion. Undoubtedly some bullies do intimidate others by using physical force, especially boys in primary schools. This approach is often used in cases of extortion. The bulk of them however are more concerned with creating an aura of dominance by projecting themselves as 'big' personalities.

It comes across in the interviews that many bullies are 'loud-mouths' insensitive to the feelings of others. Some may not even be aware of the suffering their behaviour causes as they are so caught up in their own self-aggrandisement. Ostensibly, they may do it for a 'laugh' but there is nearly always the underlying motive of increasing their status within the group. This leads on to the idea of the 'gang'. It is a common belief among students that many bullies are lacking in confidence and need the support of a 'gang' or 'group' to bolster it. In primary schools there were frequent references to bullies being cowards who pick on smaller or younger people than themselves. Thus, the school yard often becomes the arena for their activities. In secondary schools the gang may be replaced by the 'in group'. The bully has a reputation to protect and has to continually prove himself/herself in front of his/her 'friends'. Therefore, much of this behaviour can be seen as 'attention-seeking'. They have to prove they are 'somebody'. The skill of the bully lies in his/her ability to identify an appropriate 'victim'. Ideally they need somebody who can be repeatedly used to highlight their dominance. The 'best' victim is one who absorbs repeated harassment without drawing attention to the bully. People who are in some way obviously different become targets. It is a question of using the repertoire of name calling, jeering, exclusion, intimidation, physical intimidation to find the most appropriate subject. Obviously, different bullies use different methods.

There appears to be a smaller number of bullies whose behaviour is particularly disturbing. These are people who take an almost cynical pleasure in inflicting gratuitous pain on others. The pain may be physical or psychological or a combination of both. The enjoy it and get a 'kick out of it'.

Some bullies may be academically weak – the 'dossers' or 'messers'. They often have nothing else to do and their behaviour may be viewed as some form of compensation for their otherwise 'low' standing in the class.

The bullies are not really popular. In primary schools their position is often based on fear. In secondary schools they may confuse dominance with leadership. Like the victims they lack social skills but are much more adept at developing strategies to cope with this. Quite a number of students pointed to the fact that bullies may have problems at home. This can be used to explain their behaviour. In many ways the bully is a performer who needs an audience to give approval and praise. The performance often masks what is going on in the mind of a bully. He/she behaves in a very deliberate way to create situations where they are in control of others. These include both the victim(s) and the other members of the group. The underlying reasons for their behaviour can be very varied. Some may be reacting to a difficult home background where perhaps they themselves are victims. Others may be acting out of frustration at poor achievement in school. Sometimes jealousy may be the motive, of someone who does well at school or gets on well with teachers and peers. All of this makes it difficult to speak about a typical bully.

What is Bullying?
One of the most upsetting aspects of bullying is that the victim is innocent. There is no obvious reason why they should become the object of harassment. However, it is possible to explain it partly by pointing to the fact that most victims are socially isolated with few if any people in the group who would take their part. In the class there is a 'silent majority'.

They may not take any direct part in the bullying but neither do they do anything to try and stop it. They may feel uneasy but fear of the bully and his/her group usually prevents them from taking action.

Physical bullying is much more common among boys than girls. It occurs more often in primary than secondary schools. It may include pushing, shoving and/or tripping people up. Among boys there is also the phenomenon of the 'mess fight'. Teachers are familiar with the refrain 'We were only messing'. Usually, this is the case but it may also represent an opportunity for one or more students to physically harass others. This form of behaviour may be seen in school playgrounds and especially in the immediate vicinity of the school when school ends. A number of primary school students mentioned a particular ploy of bullies where they deliberately provoke the victim to the point where he/she loses his/her temper. At this stage appeal is made to the teacher and the real victim is cast in the role of bully. This experience usually ensures that the victim will react passively to any further harassment. Some bullying takes the form of intimidation. It may be physical but can also take the form of threats – 'I'll get you after school.' Particularly upsetting to victims can be the so-called 'look'. This may be a scowl or an expression which conveys aggression and/or dislike. Yet another type of bullying is where older students pick on those younger than themselves. This usually happens in the school yard.

Personal property can be the focus of attention for the bully. There may be damage to bicycles, clothes and books. The contents of school bags and pencil cases may be dumped on the floor repeatedly. Books may be stolen or hidden. Demands for money may be made often accompanied by threats. In primary schools actual lunches may be taken or lunch money stolen. Demands for money may be made, often accompanied by threats. In secondary schools which have a tuck shop, older students may demand sweets or money from younger students.

Many students would consider name-calling to be a form of bullying if it is constantly directed at the same person and if it is used to deliberately hurt or insult that person. 'Slagging' is a term used by a lot of students to indicate bullying. They were not referring to the good-hearted banter which goes on as part of the normal social interchange between people. They focussed on two aspects. The first is similar to name-calling where very personal remarks are aimed again and again at the same individual about appearance, clothes, or personal hygiene. Secondly, comments about members of family – mother, father, brother, sister could be used in a damaging way. Most often these comments have a sexual connotation.

A form of bullying known as 'isolation' can occur particularly in girls' schools. A certain person is deliberately excluded and ignored by the class group. This practice is usually initiated by the bully. It may go on for long periods of time. Other aspects of this form of behaviour may be to write insulting remarks about the person on the blackboard or in other public places, or to pass around notes about them or to whisper insults about them loud enough for them to hear. One student described what it is like to be in such a situation – 'I felt I was about an inch high.'

Where does Bullying happen?

Most bullying in primary schools takes place in the playground or outside the school (usually on the way home). The single teacher system seems to reduce bullying to a minimum in the actual classroom. The playground is a different matter. The large numbers of children thrown together, usually in a small area, create an environment very conducive to bullying. It is very difficult for teachers to monitor and control the myriad interactions which go on in a school playground. Many of the games which children play present possibilities for bullying because of their physical nature e.g. chasing, bulldog, etc.. It is relatively easy to single out and harass another child. It is in the playground that the gang can inflict physical and/or psychological damage on a victim. Children may be teased, taunted, called names or cornered. The noise level masks much of what is going on. Some children in primary school fear the playground. The area immediately outside the school often becomes an extension of the playground with the bully and his/her gang waiting for the victim and an opportunity to inflict more pain. In some schools, the toilets and the cloakrooms may be the scene of harassment. This is true of both primary and secondary schools.

In secondary schools bullying can occur in the short breaks between classes and the longer breaks throughout the day. It may also occur in class, if the teacher permits an atmosphere where comments may be made by students about their fellows. It may occur more subtly through glances, looks and sniggers. The area outside the school, or even the local shops may be the scene of bullying. Many students felt that most bullying occurs outside the school.

Some students referred to the age at which bullying problems are most likely to occur in school. In primary schools the consensus was that most bullying occurs between third and sixth classes. In secondary school it was seen as most common in first and second year with a minor peak again at the change into senior cycle. Overall it was felt that it decreases with age.

What can be done?

'If there is bullying going on in a school, can anything be done about it?' This question was the lead-in to getting students to speak about possible solutions. The bullies were certainly not intimidated by the question and many of them had practical ideas which they put forward in a very matter of fact way. Some of these were 'get the person being picked on to stand up for himself/herself', 'tell a teacher', 'tell the principal', 'change schools'. The control students were less sure. Quite a number said they did not know: 'I haven't really thought about it.' A number of others were resigned to the fact that bullying is always going to be there: 'It's human nature, isn't it?' The victims were not hopeful of change because they were afraid to tell. The fear that the bullying could get worse, especially outside school, was a major impediment to them reporting it to anyone. Furthermore, they spoke about the age-old fear of being seen as 'a rat', 'a snitch', 'a weed' or 'a grass'.

The cycle of silence can only be broken if someone does tell. However, the victim tends not to tell for the reasons given above, and because they are often unpopular and don't mix with the group, it is unlikely that anybody will come to their aid.

PART IV

Profiles of some Bullies and Victims

The following profiles have been included to indicate the variety of types of bully and victim. It is not the intention to give an example of every type because, while there may be certain common characteristics, it is not possible to speak about a typical bully or victim. Names, personal and family details have been changed in order to ensure confidentiality.

Bully 1

Ronald is an aggressive bully. He is in fifth class in a primary school. Of the five children in his family he is the second youngest. Ronald's father works as a storeman.

Ronald's attendance is average for the school. He says that he likes all of his classes except when 'they tell on you'. He likes teachers that have time for 'a few jokes' and are not 'narky'. His teacher described his school performance as poor and on occasion he has received remedial help. However, in speaking to him it was obvious that he was in no way dull. Ronald's teacher also commented that he is physically strong. In the opinion of his teacher, Ronald's parents are not friendly to deal with. Neither is Ronald close to them.

Ronald has a self-assured, relaxed personality. The vast majority of his class nominated him as someone who breaks the rules of the school and the rules of games. He emerged as an insensitive, selfish and dominating individual. One girl said she liked her class when 'I am not with Ronald ... '. However, within the class he is quite popular, especially with the boys.

When interviewed, he was polite but aloof. He thought carefully before answering the questions. There was often a contrast between his answers in the interview and some previous written answers. Asked for his opinion of fighting he said, 'I don't fight unless I have a reason.' However, his peers had rated him at the highest possible level on the extent to which he starts fights. In his opinion the people who get picked on are 'nice people'. Sometimes, people are 'just looking to be picked on'. He described bullies as 'chickens' because 'they pick on someone they can kill'. They usually pick on younger people by pushing them around and telling them what to do. These younger people may be from their own class or other classes. He felt that most bullying happened in the yard. He described how some of the other boys would get together and walk around deliberately bumping into people. When he was asked if he thought bullying was a problem in this school he said 'I wouldn't know, I haven't been bullied.'

Ronald had some very constructive suggestions about what could be done about bullying. 'The bully should be taken to the principal to explain. After that, they should not be allowed in the yard at break-time.' This logical approach contrasts with an earlier written reply, when he suggested that the best approach to dealing with the bully is to 'kick his head in'.

Ronald is an aggressive bully who intimidates and dominates others. He enjoys a certain status because of this, especially among the boys. It is probable that he is the leader of a gang. His home background would suggest that Ronald has been forced to be independent. He is very clever at disguising his behaviour, and because of this it would be difficult to prove anything against him in a school situation.

Bully 2

Brian attends a secondary school. He is a bully who feels inadequate in the school situation. The thing that annoys him about his class is that 'everybody is smarter than me'. He also wishes that he did not have to wear glasses. In addition, his form-teacher referred to the fact that he has a slight twitch near his mouth. Despite these negative aspects, he is emotionally stable, relaxed and tough-minded.

Brian is the youngest of six children and lives in a different locality to the school. His father is a taxi driver. He is not really close to either of his parents. He speaks of his mother 'going out of her way to please people'. His teacher referred to the fact that Brian is often absent when tests are on. His mother writes notes to explain these absences saying that he gets bad stomach upsets.

Brian's attitude to fighting is that he would fight if he had a good reason, not just because he knew he could beat someone. If someone tried to push him around he would 'give it to him straight between the eyes'. He describes people who get picked on as 'the weaker, ugly ones, who can't stand up for themselves'. Perceptively, he stresses the second aspect, pointing out that not all weak people are picked on. To Brian, bullies are people who like putting others down.

They do it to make others like them, because they are 'big'. Asked if bullies really are popular, Brian gave a rather off-putting chuckle and said 'actually they are usually, yeah!' He describes bullying as 'slagging for nothing, pushing and tripping'. It usually happens in the corridor after classes. His form teacher referred to the fact that it had been report-ed to him that Brian had been involved in bullying incidents in the yard.

Brian was not optimistic that anything could be done about bullying. He was of the opinion that parents and teachers can do nothing. He said 'No, there's not a lot really; you can say all you want. The teachers can do everything they can, but if it's going to happen, it's going to happen. People who are bullied do not tell because they'd get picked on even more.'

Speaking to Brian, I was struck by his composure. He is obviously concerned about his performance in school and his appearance. However, he seems to have been able to compensate for these negative aspects. He is of the opinion that he gets on well with everybody in the class. This seems to be confirmed by his peers, who rate him as quite popular.

As the youngest of six children, Brian has probably learned certain coping strategies and it is interesting that while he does not seem to approve of the fact that his mother goes out of her way to please people, he is quite willing to call on her when it suits his own needs.

Bully 3

Fiona attends a secondary school. She is the eldest of four children and finds this a big responsibility. She says 'If there's a bit of trouble it's mostly blamed on me because I should be showing good example.' Her father works as a printer. She is close to her parents. Fiona says that she likes to enjoy herself. In her opinion, her biggest fault is that she gets angry too quickly and blames somebody even if it is not their fault. She feels that her classmates think she is stupid. The thing she dislikes most about them is 'that they can be talking to you one day, but the next day, you do something wrong and nobody talks to you'.

Fiona is very conscious of what she calls 'the group in the class who do all their homework'. She says that she likes her class when they are all having a good time and getting on. In general, the class does not approve of her behaviour. One girl says, 'She shows off and everybody knows her because of her mouth.' Explaining why nobody voted for Fiona to be class captain another of her classmates says, 'They all thought she would not be good enough to be captain.' Many of the people in her class say that Fiona quarrels and gets angry and breaks the rules of the school and games. 'She always wants a fight,' is how another girl views her.

That her behaviour is outside the norms for the class is suggested by the following statement: 'She is too loud and uses bad and rude language.'

The results of her tests and answers to her questionnaires show that Fiona is careless of social rules and excessively boastful and attention seeking. She wants to make an impression by showing off. Her attitude to fighting is that 'It's OK now and again'. She suggests that the people who get picked on at school are the ones who 'work really hard all the time'. The people who pick on them get a kick out of it – a laugh. She also says that sometimes they are jealous'. People bully these students by not talking to them or maybe taking their things. She says that people like this do not tell somebody, but keep it all bottled up, because they are afraid of worse trouble.

Fiona is a bully who suffers from an inferiority complex. She does not 'fit in' in her class group but desperately wants to be accepted. She focuses her dislike and frustration on those who are most unlike herself. They are the easy targets. By dominating them she is trying to build up her own status, but most of the time it has the reverse effect, making her more unpopular and more isolated.

Victim 1

Joan is in fifth class in a primary school. Unknown to herself she is a provocative victim. She comes from a family of five children and is in the middle. Her father is a solicitor. Joan does not like school very much. She is absent more than the average for the school. Her teacher said Joan often complains of tummy aches and headaches. Ten people in the class of thirty-three selected her as the person that no one wants to work with. Her peers rated her as very unpopular and a definite aggression target. Some of the boys described her as 'fat' and 'ugly'. Her teacher referred to the fact that Joan has poor co-ordination and fidgets a lot.

In terms of behaviour, she seeks unwittingly to gain attention. She also irritates the class at lunch time by her eating habits. One pupil describes how Joan 'makes slurping noises'. Joan has very low self esteem. She is very insecure and given to worrying. This often shows itself in her excitable nature where she is over-active and attention seeking. She is very close to her parents. In fact her teacher describes her behaviour as 'babyish' and attributes it to the fact that her mother is 'over-protective'. The teacher has spoken to Joan's mother, asking her to get Joan to do jobs on her own, e.g. go to the shop alone. She feels this approach could make Joan less immature. However, there is also pressure on Joan at home. She says that if she does not do well in the tests each week she is 'in big trouble'.

Joan is well aware that she is unpopular in her class. They call her a 'nerd' and make remarks about her clothes. She is of the opinion that the main reason she is picked on is because she used to wear a hearing aid. She describes how most of her class think they are better than her. She speaks about having had three friends throughout her time in school but that 'they dumped her'. She gets angry when people make fun of her. She feels she is picked on because 'she does her own thing'.

She thinks that bullies are 'mean and laugh a lot. They think they're great. They want to get something out of you – make you chase them or be afraid of them.' When she is called names she feels horrible and sad, and wishes she were someone else. She says she would not tell on the bullies because 'they'll be in school the next day and sometimes the teacher will not be watching.'

Joan is a very sensitive, insecure child. She does not really know why she is picked on. She uses the excuse of the hearing aid, which she no longer uses, as a crutch. The real reason is that she is physically unattractive and has some annoying personal habits. Her sensitivity and her protected home background have made her very isolated.

Victim 2

Paul is in fourth year of a secondary school. In the year in which he sat his Intermediate Certificate he was in the top stream class of four classes. There are five children in his family and he is the eldest. Being the eldest was a source of great pressure for Paul in relation to his examination. His parents expected 'a lot of him'. His father works as a salesman.

The ratings of his peers indicated that Paul is a very unpopular student and a definite target for aggression. Of the twenty-eight students in Paul's class, twenty-five nominated him as the person in the class that no one wanted to work with. In giving the reason why, the language and tone indicated a level of dislike and contempt which is disturbing. He was called a 'swot' and a 'teacher's pet'. One student put it this way: 'He's a teacher's pet and a yes sir, no sir, three bags full sir type.' The atmosphere of the class seemed to indicate that it is unacceptable to work too hard, or to have too close a relationship with teachers.

One student said that if you worked with Paul, you would be slagged yourself. When the atmosphere in a class is dictated and dominated by very aggressive individuals this attitude is common. Most ironic was the statement of the student who said, 'He's a proper prat, but no one lets on that we don't like him.'

In terms of personality, Paul is sober, serious and sensitive but there is also a large measure of attention-seeking in his behaviour. In the course of his interview, Paul described in great detail the events on three occasions when he says that he retaliated in a very physical way to intimidation and provocation. All the evidence from his questionnaires, tests, teachers and peers suggests that he does not react in this way. Perhaps this is what he would like to have done.

Paul has been a victim over a long period of time. He has been bullied in primary and secondary school, by a number of different people. He has been subjected to many forms of bullying – physical, verbal, extortion, and destruction of personal property. Destruction of personal property could be illustrated by his tale of how a student smeared ink all over his books. He was subjected to physical violence when cornered in the yard. The depth of his distress was shown when he described his aggressor as having given him 'so much pain'.

As a result of being bullied Paul has been depressed at various time. From time to time, he was absent from school. Often, even when he was present, he was unable to concentrate.

Eventually, when Paul was in third year, things became so bad that out of desperation he confided in a teacher. The teacher investigated Paul's reports of name–calling, intimidation, and damage to property. The people responsible were identified and severely punished. The teacher continues to monitor the situation carefully. It is encouraging to see that there has been a major improvement in Paul's life. This particular case supports strongly the argument for intervention but raises the question of a definite school policy with regard to bullying behaviour.

Victim 3

Ross goes to a secondary school. He has a younger sister. He feels very negative about his father who works on a casual basis and is very aggressive. He is close to and respects his mother. Although his peers feel that he is a very definite aggression target, they do not rate him as unpopular. However, Ross has very low self esteem and keeps very much to himself. One of his tests indicated that he is 'jumpy' and easily scared. In interviewing him, I noticed that he fidgeted continuously without seeming to realise it. His school attendance is below average.

Asked about his class, Ross said that the things about it that annoy him are the slagging and the bullying, 'Occasionally some of the slagging goes a bit far.' Explaining this he went on to say that the whole class calls him 'carrot head'. This name started when he was in primary school. Most of the class do it 'to get on his nerves'. Ross has very red hair and a pale complexion. He says that he gets angry when he is bullied and teachers shout at him. He is of the opinion that the people in his class think he is a 'shithead'. If he could change himself, he would like to be 'popular and respected'. He finds it difficult to make friends. He likes his class when they are friendly with him.

Ross does not like fighting. He feels that the kind of people

76

who get picked on are 'like me, because I'm not one of the lads'. Bullies are 'people who do what they like, for a laugh'.

It struck me as unusual that Ross was considered academically weak because it was clear from his tests and questionnaires and from talking to him, that he has a quick intelligence. His home background would seem to have made him insecure. His difficulty in making and keeping friends increases this insecurity. It upsets him that his classmates pick on him and call him names. It is probable that they are unaware of the distress it causes him. Because he is not unpopular, this name-calling is probably not vindictive. However, because Ross lacks confidence and is very sensitive, it upsets him greatly, but he does not show it.

PART V

Preventive and Treatment Approaches

Parents

The basis of a good relationship is communication. Parents should endeavour to create an atmosphere where their child will speak openly to them, even about matters which they find very upsetting. Fear and shame are the main impediments to children confiding in their parents if they are being bullied. There are two aspects to this fear. Firstly, the child is afraid that any approach to the school by the parent will make the situation worse. Secondly, there is the deepseated fear of being seen as a 'rat' by his/her peers. The shame the victim feels is related to a belief that he/she must have done something to deserve this harassment or intimidation.

The child who is a victim will seldom speak openly about it. Rather they will drop hints, or show by their general demeanour that something is wrong. Young children may make comments about the fact that it is very crowded in the playground or that someone is always chasing them. Older children may let slip that they really dislike a particular person. It may be as vague as 'John is a pain'. The following 'observations' could possibly indicate to a parent that their child is being bullied at school:

    1. A child who has been happy at school losing interest and enthusiasm for school. This may be reflected in a deterioration in school performance.

2. Requests for parents to drive them to school, or collect them, even though the school is within walking distance.

3. Damage to bicycles or personal property, e.g. clothes, books, or loss of same.

4. A child returning from school in very bad humour but reluctant to say why.

5. Unexplained changes of mood. These will often occur before the restart of school, e.g. at the end of a weekend, or the end of holidays.

6. Frequent minor illnesses, especially headaches and tummyaches. These often accompany the mood changes mentioned above.

7. An increase in requests for money. If refused this may provoke angry outbursts.

8. Unexplained cuts or bruises.

If a parent discovers that any of the above are the result of bullying, definite action should be taken. Firstly, full details of what has been happening should be obtained from the child. They should be written down with a record of dates and times if possible. Many parents of victims also feel ashamed that their child has been bullied. This can provoke questions about what they have done wrong. The first approach should be to the class teacher. Depending on the attitude of the class teacher, it may be necessary to go to the principal. The most important thing is to provide support for the child on an on-going basis. In the case of older children, parents should contact the school counsellor (if there is one) in order to widen the support group. Parents should also explore the possibility that their child may have provoked bullying. For example, I have found that, in some cases, poor personal hygiene can be an initial cause of victimisation. Sometimes provocative behaviour can cause a child to be bullied.

It is much easier to get younger children to speak about bullying. Older children may hide the problem from their parents for years. Hence, there is a need to develop good communication when children are younger, so that it is in place if required later on. The role of the parent in helping the victim is crucial, especially if the child is at secondary school. Because there are so many teachers involved with each class group, the problem can occur unknown to teachers. Often the parent is the only one who can make the first move. A parent should never agree with their child to keep the bullying a secret.

Sometimes, a parent may have the unpleasant experience of being informed by their child's teacher or principal that he/she has been involved in bullying. The parent should try to find out why their child is bullying. They should ensure that their child apologises to the child he/she bullied. Some children become temporary bullies after a traumatic event, such as separation of parents or the birth of a new baby. Others may be bored or frustrated. They need help to feel good about themselves and the parents can often be the best people to do this. An indication to parents that their child may be a bully at school may be the manner in which the child relates to his/her brothers/sisters. A child who is permanently aggressive and insensitive in the home environment is quite possibly a bully at school. Parents should be on the look out for verbal as well as physical abrasiveness. This behaviour may even extend to the parents themselves, usually the mother.

Teachers are well aware that the parents of many bullies will not accept that their child has been involved in bullying. It is also the case that the behaviour of many of these parents may be the main cause of the child bullying. In very serious cases of bullying, the school principal may have no option but to contact the police.

Principals

The principal has the key role in dealing with bullying behaviour in school, because he/she is in a position to set standards on the issue. The starting point could be to draw up an explicit, clearly defined school policy to deal with bullying behaviour. This policy could be drawn up in consultation with the staff. Initially, the staff may need to meet a number of times as there are usually varying opinions about this behaviour and how it should be handled. The intention should be to reach a consensus about how bullying in the school will be treated. Ideally, the policy could be in written form and take its place with other items on the school rules such as uniforms, punctuality, and so on. The parents and the student body should be aware of the school's attitude to bullying. In interviewing the parents of incoming students, the principal could explain the school's policy on bullying so that the parents are aware of procedures and sanctions should their child becomes involved in this behaviour.

Each spring in secondary schools it is usual for the principal or the school counsellor to meet with the principals and teachers of the feeder schools. This presents an opportunity to obtain information about incoming children who might be 'at risk' from bullying, as well as other general information. Individual teachers of sixth classes would be in the best position to supply this information. It is not advisable to look for information about children who might be bullies. The label could be inaccurate or unjustified.

From time to time at assembly, the principal could reiterate the school's attitude to this behaviour. The principal should treat seriously all approaches from parents regarding bullying. Written records should be kept of any such meetings. Given the demanding nature of the principal's day, it would be impossible for him/her to deal directly with all students who may have been bullies. Therefore, the school should have a structure to deal with incidents of bullying behaviour.

The school playground is the scene of a lot of bullying, especially in primary schools. School principals can take practical steps to improve the situation. I have found that much of the bullying in the playground takes the form of older children picking on younger children. 'Gangs' are often involved. In many primary schools the younger children, e.g. up to third class, have their own play area, as have the older children (4th to 6th class). If this were common practice in all primary schools, the amount of bullying should decrease.

Increased supervision throughout schools would also improve the situation. However, at a time when the workload of teachers is increasing significantly, this suggestion may not seem practical. If bullying is common in a school, it is certain to affect the overall atmosphere. In the classroom it may make the teacher's job more difficult in terms of maintaining a standard of discipline. In addition, the more relaxed atmosphere created by an absence of tension between students will also benefit teachers.If a school wishes to ascertain how serious a problem bullying behaviour is, anonymous questionnaires could be given to all students. This could be organised by form tutors in secondary schools. The questionnaire could include questions about the year in which the student is, what they consider bullying to be, if they have ever been bullied. If the answer is yes, where did it happen and was it reported? If it wasn't reported, why not? It could conclude by asking what the school can do about bullying.

Such a questionnaire could be as detailed as the staff wishses and, because it is anonymous, it could be the source of very accurate information about the extent of the problem.

Teachers

At the outset, it is necessary to emphasise that a teacher's primary task is very demanding. To suggest that teachers are solely responsible for the prevention or eradication of bullying behaviour in schools would be inaccurate. That so many of them are interested in doing so is a tribute to their interest in the children they teach.

In primary schools, it is important that a child who is picked on feels confident about approaching his/her teacher. The intention should be to create what is often referred to as a 'telling school', i.e. where people feel free to speak to those in authority without fear of the stigma of being called a 'rat'. It is vital that all matters reported to a teacher are investigated fully and confidentially and followed up if necessary. There can be few things more damaging for a child than to confide in someone they believe can help them and to receive only temporary help. When this happens the fundamental fear of many victims will be realised when the bully intensifies harassment. Victims will feel even more frightened and isolated than before.

It may be that a child in a class reports to a teacher that somebody is being harassed by one or more children, giving names. In this situation, a teacher could approach one of the bullies, saying that they saw something nasty happening, perhaps in the yard. They could stress that nobody told them this and that they hope that it will not happen again. One bully usually relays this message to any other bullies. Because the teacher has not spoken to the victim, the victim's anonymity is protected.

Such an approach is not usually suitable for more serious cases of bullying. In serious cases, the victim needs the direct support of the teacher on an on-going basis. Once again, this could be done in a low-key rather than a public way.

Sometimes a teacher may unwittingly instigate bullying by repeatedly singling out the same child for praise, or asking the same child to do 'jobs' for them. This may have the effect of attracting negative attention to the child from a jealous bully in the class. Such a person may turn the majority of the class against this child who may come to be seen as a teacher's 'pet' or 'lick'. This behaviour will usually go on as part of the 'hidden agenda' of the class. The child who is the victim is virtually powerless to do anything because they find it difficult to explain to a teacher that they don't want to be the centre of attention.

In secondary schools it is possible to develop a tiered structure for dealing with bullying behaviour. It begins with the class subject teachers, then goes to the form masters/ mistresses. At the next stage is the counsellor, with the principal at the top. The form teacher has the advantage of knowing the group well and would be in a position to offer support if necessary. Class teachers who come across incidents of bullying, either in class or around the school in general, need to get the names of the people involved. The nature of the incident and the people involved should be reported to the appropriate form teacher. The form teacher now takes responsibility for investigating the incident fully. A written record should be kept. The form teacher has a number of options on how to approach the problem.

(a) Speak to the class of the bully (bullies) and victim(s) pointing out the injustice and undesirability of this behaviour.

(b) Speak separately to the bully (bullies) and victim(s) pointing out the injustice and undesirability of this behaviour.

(c) Confront the bully (bullies) with the victim(s) without others present and initiate a discussion on what the victim felt like when bullied.

The first approach tends not to have any lasting effect because of the security a bully usually enjoys within a stable group. Generally, it is not a good idea to appeal publicly to the class group to support a victim. Very often this kind of public attention increases the discomfort of the victim. It may also serve to confirm the 'victim' status of a student. Some bullies also enjoy this kind of public exposure of a victim. The best approach seems to be (b) followed by (c). The separate interviews with the bully and the victim will enable the teacher to form an opinion on the personalities of the students concerned. A discussion between the bully and the victim often has the effect of making a bully realise the full impact of his/her actions. However, if the bullying has been severe and ongoing, the victim may feel unable to face the bully. The teacher is best advised to suggest this only when he she senses that the victim is confident enough to proceed. If a group of students is involved it can be a time consuming procedure, but it usually brings results. A follow-up

89

meeting with the teacher who reported the incident helps keep all parties informed of any developments and encourages teachers to report incidents of bullying behaviour.

Particularly serious cases of bullying should be referred to the principal. It may be necessary to contact parents but this should be the responsibility of the principal.

Teachers should ensure that they do not unwittingly instigate or confirm bullying behaviour. The so called 'provocative victim' is usually a source of irritation to teachers as well as to his/her peers. In the eyes of the bully (bullies) constant reprimand and/or criticism of such an individual by the teacher may legitimise and confirm their victim status.

Some children have a particular expression or nervous twitch which may get them into trouble with teachers. It may sometimes appear as if they are sneering or grinning at a teacher. If there has been tension between a teacher and a class, the teacher may misinterpret such a pupil's expression. What appears to be insolence may just be their natural expression or a nervous reaction.

From time to time a teacher may stumble upon the 'hidden agenda' of group dynamics within a class. In some situations, it may be necessary to divide the class into groups, e.g. in home economics or at five-a-side football in P.E.. Sometimes there is a student with whom no one wants to work. This person may have been isolated by the class group for any number of reasons. In the class, the teacher may have to insist that the pupil be allowed to join a particular group, but afterwards it may well prove worthwhile to interview privately and discreetly either the isolated person or some student in the class whom the teacher knows well. Occasionally it will emerge that bullying has been going on within that group.

In secondary schools, teachers may also use their own subjects to initiate a discussion on bullying in a non-contrived way. For English teachers, *Lord of the Flies* can be most useful in this context. In history, there is a long list of dictators who could give rise to a discussion. In geography, colonisation illustrates many aspects of domination and exploitation.

The School Counsellor

The school counsellor is in a position to help both bullies and victims. The principal can refer serious cases of bullying to the counsellor, having taken the appropriate disciplinary 'action'. Ideally, the counsellor should be seen as a facilitator within a school community. The idea of community suggests that its members have rights and responsibilities. In this context, the victim has a right to freedom from bullying behaviour and the bully must be made to take responsibility for his/her actions. Discussions with the bully and the victim can enable the counsellor to work towards achieving this situation.

The counsellor also has a role in the rehabilitation of the bully and the victim. The bully often has problems at home or in school. The victim may not even know why he/she is being bullied. The counsellor can help both initially just by listening. A practical way to help the victim is by helping him/her develop more positive body language, e.g. making eye contact with people more frequently. The student should be encouraged to enter the classroom with head and shoulders upright. It may take some time to achieve results with this approach. There will be setbacks. Consequently, the continuing support of the counsellor is vital.

The victim should also be encouraged to take more interest in others. I have found that many of them are isolated. They therefore lack support in times of difficulty. They should take more interest in others. Perhaps there is someone in the class with whom they feel they have something in common. Often the bully has low self esteem. The counsellor can help by making the bully feel more positive about himself/ herself. Many bullies have no interest in school. Outside school they may have no hobbies or interests. At home there may be nobody to take any real interest in them. The counsellor can encourage them to become more involved in school life (e.g. sport). It is important for the counsellor to suggest to the bully that a change in his/her pattern of behaviour could lead to a much happier life in school.

The bullies and the victims need help on an on-going long-term basis. The investment of time on the part of the counsellor is immense. If too many people arrive for counselling, the system will soon become over-loaded. The form teachers should endeavour to ensure that only the most serious cases go to the counsellor.

Teacher Training
Principals and teachers indicated in their questionnaires that they do not feel that teacher training had adequately prepared them to deal with the problem of bullying behaviour in schools. Perhaps, education departments in the universities and the teacher training colleges could include a section on bullying in schools as part of their courses.

The Role of Senior Students

In some schools, each September either fifth or sixth years (or both, depending on numbers) are given special responsibility for the new first years. The idea is to help the first year students through the difficult early weeks where so much is new. The relationship between the older and the younger students should ideally be such that the younger students will feel able to confide in the older ones of necessary. This can be an important means of combatting bullying because a young student might approach a trusted older student rather than confide in a teacher. The information could then be passed discreetly to the relevant form teacher who would then take responsibility for dealing with it.

Non-teaching Staff

Just as the P.E. teacher will often see very different behaviour from what the ordinary class teacher sees, so also will other staff in a school. Kitchen staff, office staff, gardeners, janitors and lollipop men and women will witness bullying behaviour. In a 'telling' school they will feel confident about approaching the principal or vice-principal to report what they have seen. Their approaches should be taken seriously, because they are also part of the school community.

School Buses
There have been increasing reports of bullying on private school buses. Responsibility for dealing with this behaviour lies primarily with the bus driver, but if necessary he should forward names to the school principal.